POVERTY OF SPIRIT

POVERTY
OF
SPIRIT

by
Johannes Baptist Metz

Translated by
John Drury

PAULIST PRESS
Paramus, N.J.   New York, N.Y.

Contents

A Paulist Press Edition, originally published under the title *Armut im geiste* by Verlag Ars Sacra Josef Müller, Munich, W. Germany. NIHIL OBSTAT: Rev. Robert E. Hunt, S.T.D., *Censor Librorum*, IMPRIMATUR: ✠ Thomas A. Boland, S.T.D., *Archbishop of Newark*, March 19, 1968. © 1968 by The Missionary Society of St. Paul the Apostle in the State of New York, Library of Congress Catalog Card Number: 68-31045. Published by **Paulist Press**, *Editorial Office:* 1865 Broadway, N.Y., N.Y. 10023, *Business Office:* Paramus, New Jersey 07652. Printed and bound in the United States of America.

ISBN: 0-8091-1924-2

Foreword

Becoming a human being involves more than conception and birth. It is a mandate and a mission, a command and a decision. A human being has an open-ended relationship to himself. He does not possess his being unchallenged; he cannot take his being for granted as God does his. Nor does he possess it in the same way as the other creatures around him. Other animals, for example, survive in mute innocence and cramped necessity. With no future horizons, they are what they are from the start; the law of their life and being is spelled out for them, and they resign themselves to these limits without question.

Man, however, is challenged and questioned from the depths of his boundless spirit. Being is entrusted to him as a summons, which he is to accept and consciously acknowledge. He is never simply a being that is "there" and "ready-made", just for the asking. From the very start he is something that can Be, a being who must win his selfhood and decide what he is to be. He must fully *become* what he *is*—a human being. To become man through the exercise of his freedom—that is the law of his Being.

Now this freedom, which leaves us to ourselves, is not pure arbitrariness or unchecked whim; it is not devoid of law and necessity. It reveals itself at work when we accept and approve with all our heart the being that is committed to us, when we make it so much our own that it seems to be our idea from the first. The inescapable "truth" of our Being is such that it makes our freedom possible rather than threatening it (cf. Jn. 8, 32). Thus the free process of becoming a human being unfolds as a process of service. In biblical terms it is "obedience" (cf. Phil. 2, 8) and faithfulness to the humanity entrusted to us.

However, this process of freely becoming a man has its own inherent temptation. By its very nature this process is a trial; imbedded in it is the danger of going awry. Man, entrusted with the task of making himself man, faces danger at every side. He is always a potential rebel. He can secretly betray the humanity entrusted to him, and he has done precisely this from the very beginning (the first human beings refused to embrace the Being entrusted to them). He can try to run away from himself, from the burdens and the difficulties of his lot, even going so far as to take his own life. Under the myriad evasions of a materialistic Docetism he can "stifle" the truth of his Being (cf. Rom. 1, 18). In short he can fail to obey this truth, thus aborting his work of becoming a human being.

On the other hand, man may withstand this temptation and lovingly accept the truth of his Being. For the moment we shall call this attitude "love of self". Here we might glimpse the deep and positive significance of an attitude whose ethical and religious scope is usually overlooked and underrated, even when we use the eyes of faith. Understood correctly, man's love for himself, his "yes" to his self, may be regarded as the "categorical imperative" of the Christian faith: You shall lovingly accept the humanity entrusted to you! You shall be obedient to your destiny! You shall not continually try to escape it! You shall be true to yourself! You shall embrace yourself!

Man's self-acceptance is the basis of the Christian creed. Assent to God starts in man's sincere assent to himself, just as sinful flight from God starts in man's flight from himself. In accepting the chalice of his existence, man shows his obedience to the will of his Father in heaven (cf. Mt. 26, 39.42); in rejecting it, he rejects God. Knowing the temptation which humanity itself is, knowing how readily man tries to escape the

harsh distress of the human situation, knowing
how difficult it is for him to bear with himself
and how quickly he feels betrayed by himself,
knowing how difficult it is for man not to hate
himself (as Bernanos points out), we can then
understand why God had to prescribe "self-love"
as a virtue and one of the great commandments.
We can then understand why we constantly
need the help of his grace. We can then realize
how much easier it is to say "no" instead of
"yes" to oneself, and why all asceticism is first
designed to serve this great "yes".

Man must learn to accept himself in the painful experiment of his living. He must embrace
the spiritual adventure of becoming a man,
moving through the many stages that lie between birth and death. Even the life of the child
is darkened by the repulsive enigma of death.
Soon enough, with man's first feeble explora-
tions into the unchartered inner depths of his
personality, is he tempted to an outright denial
of what is most his own. Man's flight from himself begins early.

God "became man"; he took on our flesh. We
say this all too casually, because inadvertently
we are accustomed to consider only the biologi-
cal event, the external process. But the assumption of man's type of Being is primarily a spirit-

ual venture pulsing through the free activity of our heart. It is an unfolding story, an inner journey; it commences with conception and birth, but these events do not tell the whole story.

God becomes man: What are the spiritual lineaments of this process? What does it involve? What motivations lie behind it? Paul describes it in a famous passage (Phil. 2, 5-11). The Synoptics also have something to say about it, describing its inner thrust in the story of Jesus' temptation in the desert. Unless we are greatly mistaken, this story is the biblical way of presenting the spiritual process involved in God's assumption of humanity.

GOD
BECOMES
MAN

Then Jesus was led up by the Spirit into the wilderness to be tempted by the devil. And he fasted forty days and forty nights, and afterward he was hungry. And the tempter came and said to him, "If you are the Son of God, command these stones to become loaves of bread." But he answered, "It is written, 'Man shall not live by bread alone, but by every word that proceeds from the mouth of God'" (Deut. 8, 3).

Then the devil took him to the holy city, and set him on the pinnacle of the temple, and said to him, "If you are the Son of God, throw yourself down; for it is written, 'He will give his angels charge of you,' and 'On their hands they will bear you up, lest you strike your foot against a stone'" (Ps. 90, 11-12).

Jesus said to him, "Again it is written, 'You shall not tempt the Lord your God'" (Deut. 6, 16).

Again the devil took him to a very high mountain, and showed him all the kingdoms of the world and the glory of them; and he said to him, "All these I will give you, if you will fall

down and worship me." Then Jesus said to him,
"Begone, Satan! for it is written, 'You shall worship the Lord your God and him only shall you
serve' " (Deut. 6, 13).

Then the devil left him, and behold, angels
came and ministered to him (Mt. 4, 1-11).

Let us overlook the external process involved
in these temptations; let us try to focus on their
underlying intention, on the basic strategy at
work. We can then say that the three temptations represent three assaults on the "poverty" of
Jesus, on the self-renunciation through which he
chose to redeem us. They represent an assault on
the radical and uncompromising step he has
taken: to come down from God and become
man.

To become man means to become "poor", to
have nothing which one might brag about before God. To become man means to have no
support and no power, save the enthusiasm and
commitment of one's own heart. Becoming man
involves proclaiming the poverty of the human
spirit in the face of the total claims of a transcendent God.

With the courageous acceptance of such poverty, the divine epic of our salvation began.
Jesus held back nothing; he clung to nothing,
and nothing served as a shield for him. Even his

true origin did not shield him: "He . . . did not count equality with God a thing to be grasped, but emptied himself" (Phil. 2, 6).

Satan, however, tries to obstruct this self-renunciation, this thoroughgoing "poverty". He wants to make Jesus strong, for what he really fears is the powerlessness of God in the humanity he has assumed. He fears the trojan horse of an open human heart that will remain true to its native poverty, suffer the misery and abandonment that is man's, and thus save mankind. Satan's temptation is an assault on God's self-renunciation, an enticement to strength, security and spiritual abundance; for these things will obstruct God's saving approach to man in the dark robes of frailty and weakness.

Satan tries to appeal to the divinity in Jesus; he tempers with the gravity and grandeur of his humanity. (As a matter of fact, Satan always tries to stress the spiritual strength of man and his divine character. He has done this from the beginning. "You will be like God": that is Satan's slogan. It is *the* temptation he has set before men in countless variations, urging us to reject the truth about the humanity we have been given.)

Satan joins hands with Docetism and Monophysitism. He wants God to remain simply God. He wants the Incarnation to be an empty show, where God dresses up in human costume but doesn't really commit himself to this role. He wants to make the Incarnation a piece of mythology, a divine puppet show. That is his strategy for making sure that the earth remains exclusively his, and man too. Even before man really woke up to his freedom, Satan began his assault, wooing man with soft words or confusing him with his wiles. As a result man was never impartially summoned to personal decision.

"You're hungry," he tells Jesus. "You need be hungry no longer. You can change all that with a miracle. You stand trembling on a pinnacle, overlooking a dark abyss. You need no longer put up with this frightening experience, this dangerous plight; you can command the angels to protect you from falling . . ." Satan's temptation calls upon Jesus to remain strong like God, to stand within a protecting circle of angels, to hang on to his divinity (Phil. 2, 6). He urges Jesus not to plunge into the loneliness and futility that is a real part of human existence. He urges him to flee from the desert (the prototype of man's abject poverty), to sneak away from our miserable lot that cries out to heaven. For hunger becomes a human hunger only when it can never be fully allayed; desire becomes a human desire only when it can remain unfulfilled. And nearness to the abyss becomes a human experience only when one can no longer call upon helping hands for protection.

Thus the temptation in the desert would have Jesus betray humanity in the name of God (or, diabolically, God in the name of man). Jesus' "no" to Satan is his "yes" to our poverty. He did not cling to his divinity. He did not simply dip into our existence, wave the magic wand of divine life over us, and then hurriedly retreat to his eternal home. He did not leave us with a tattered dream, letting us brood over the mystery of our existence.

Instead, Jesus subjected himself to our plight. He immersed himself in our misery and followed man's road to the end. He did not escape from the torment of our life, nobly repudiating man. With the full weight of his divinity he descended into the abyss of human existence, penetrating its darkest depths. He was not spared from the dark mystery of our poverty as human beings.

Here was a man who was "tempted as we are, yet without sinning" (Heb. 4, 15). And sin does not heighten the saga or the suffering of our uncertain plight; instead, it compromises and mitigates them. Enmeshed in sin, we do not drink in our poverty down to the last drop; we do not stare it full in the face. By sinning we make a secret compromise with the offspring of sin—the forces of suffering and death; we join forces with them before they can assault us and make us truly poor.

Christ, the sinless one, experienced the poverty of human existence more deeply and more excruciatingly than any other man could. He saw its many faces, including those shadowy aspects we never glimpse. In the poverty of his passion, he had no consolation, no companion angels, no guiding star, no Father in heaven. All he had was his own lonely heart, bravely facing its ordeal even as far as the cross (Phil. 2, 8).

Have we really understood the impoverishment that Christ endured? Everything was taken from him during the passion, even the love that drove him to the cross. No longer did he savor his own love, no longer did he feel any spark of enthusiasm. His heart gave out and a feeling of utter helplessness came over him. Truly, he emptied himself (Phil. 2, 7). God's merciful hand no longer sustained him. His countenance was hidden during the passion, and Christ gaped into the darkness of nothingness and abandonment where God was no longer present. The Son of Man reached his destiny, stretched taut between a despising earth that had rejected him and a faceless heaven thundering God's "no" to sinful mankind. Jesus paid the price of futility. He became utterly poor.

In this total renunciation, however, Jesus perfected and proclaimed in action what took place in the depths of his being: he professed and accepted our humanity, he took on and endured our lot, he stepped down from his divinity. He came to us where we really are—with all our broken dreams and lost hopes, with the meaning of existence slipping through our fingers. He came and stood with us, struggling with his whole heart to have us say "yes" to our innate poverty.

God's fidelity to man is what gives man the courage to be true to himself. And the legacy of his total commitment to mankind, the proof of his fidelity to our poverty, is the cross. The cross is the sacrament of poverty of spirit, the sacrament of authentic humanness in a sinful world. It is the sign that one man remained true to his humanity, that he accepted it in full obedience.

Hanging in utter weakness on the cross, Christ revealed the divine meaning of man's Being. It said something for the Jews and pagans that they found the cross scandalous and foolish (1 Cor. 1, 23). To the enlightened humanitarians and liberals of a later day the cross provokes only flat irony or weary skepticism. These self-styled advocates of humanity are more experienced; they are too indifferent to find the cross scandalous, yet not so naive to laugh at its foolishness. And what is it to us? Well, no one is exempted from the poverty of the cross; there is no guarantee against its intrusion. The antipathy to it found its way into the very midst of Christ's disciples: "You will all fall away because of me this night" (Mt. 26, 31).

Judas' betrayal may have been the result of frenzied impatience with Jesus' poverty, or a futile attempt to pressure Jesus into using his divine resources instead of accepting human impotence. In any case, it is not an isolated instance. Poverty of spirit is always betrayed most by those who are closest to it. It is the disciples of Christ in the Church who criticize and subvert it most savagely.

Perhaps that is why Jesus related the parable of the wheat grain. Finding in it a lesson for himself, he passed it on to his Church, so that she might remember it down through the ages, especially when the poverty intrinsic to human existence became repugnant: "Unless a grain of wheat falls into the earth and dies, it remains alone; but if it dies, it bears much fruit" (Jn. 12, 24).

MAN
BECOMES
MAN

away in his presence but assume their own proper value.

God has come to us in grace. He has endowed us with his life, and made our life his. In doing this, he did not mitigate or eliminate our innate poverty; he actually intensified it and outdid it. His grace does not cause estrangement and excess, as sin does. It reveals the full depths of our destiny (resulting from God's salvific initiative in history), which we could not have imagined by ourselves.

A man with grace is a man who has been emptied, who stands impoverished before God, who has nothing of which he can boast: "For God is at work in you, both to will and to work for his good pleasure" (Phil. 2, 13). He works out his salvation in the poverty of "fear and trembling" (Phil. 2, 12). Grace does not erase our poverty; it transforms it totally, allowing it to share in the poverty of Jesus' own immolated heart (cf. Rom. 8, 17).

This poverty, then, is not just another virtue —one among many. It is a necessary ingredient in any authentic Christian attitude toward life. Without it there can be no Christianity and no imitation of Christ. It is no accident that "poverty of spirit" is the first of the beatitudes. What is the sorrow of those who mourn, the suffering of the persecuted, the self-forgetfulness of the

merciful, or the humility of the peacemakers—
what are these if not variations of spiritual poverty? This spirit is also the mother of the three-
fold mystery of faith, hope and charity. It is the
doorway through which men must pass to become authentic human beings.

Only through poverty of spirit do men draw
near to God; only through it does God draw
near to man. Poverty of spirit is the meeting
point of heaven and earth, the mysterious place
where God and man encounter each other, the
point where infinite mystery meets concrete
existence.

The Innate
Poverty of Man

When we encounter Jesus Christ, we become sharply aware of our innate poverty as human beings. We see then the dire want of a man who lives on the bread of eternity, whose food is to do the will of the Father (cf. Jn. 4, 34). Did not Jesus live in continual dependence on Someone else? Was not his very existence hidden in the mysterious will of the Father? Was he not so thoroughly poor that he had to go begging for his very personality from the transcendent utterance of the Father? Was not his whole life buried in the mysterious will of his Father?

We are all beggars. We are all members of a species that is not sufficient unto itself. We are all creatures plagued by unending doubts and restless, unsatisfied hearts. Of all creatures, we are the poorest and the most incomplete. Our needs are always beyond our capacities, and we only find ourselves when we lose ourselves.

We cannot rest content in ourselves. In the elements and experiences of our life, to which we give meaning, we do not find satisfying light and protective security. We only find these things in the intangible mystery that overshadows our heart from the first day of our lives, awakening questions and wonderment and luring us beyond ourselves. We surrender ourselves to this mystery, as a person in love surrenders to the mystery of his beloved and there finds rest. Man is a creature whose being is sheltered and protected only insofar as he opens himself up to intangible, greater realities. He is at peace in the open, unconquered precincts of mystery.

If man leaves his dreamy conceptions aside and focuses on his naked poverty, when the masks fall and the core of his Being is revealed, it soon becomes obvious that he is religious "by nature", that religion is the secret dowry of his being. In the midst of his existence there unfolds the bond (*re-ligio*) which ties him to the infinitely transcendent mystery of God, the insatiable interest in the Absolute that captivates him and underlines his poverty.

At the core of his existence a "transcendental neediness" holds sway. It spurs and supports all his longings and desires, works itself out through them, but is never exhausted by them. When they are fulfilled it ruthlessly exposes how pro-

visional they were. It contemns man to a restless pilgrimage through the universe in search
of a final satisfaction, an "Amen," which the
poor know is theirs only in "the kingdom of
heaven" (cf. Mt. 5, 3).

The unending nature of our poverty as human beings is man's only innate treasure. He
is unlimited indigence since his very self-
possession, the integrity and lucidity of his
coming-to-Being, spring not from himself but
from the intangible mystery of God. The ultimate meaning of man is hidden in God. Man
is the *ecstatic appearance of Being,* and becoming man is an ever growing appropriation of
this ecstasis of Being. This demands an attentive
receptivity and obedient assent to the total
claim and inescapable quandry which the mystery of God poses to his human existence.

Although man does not choose to be religious
or non-religious in regard to his innermost
Being, nonetheless he is faced with the choice
implied in self-acceptance or self-alienation. He
can surrender to the ecstatic poverty of his Being, through "poverty of spirit" abiding in it.
This acceptance can reach the heights of mysticism, where through grace the human spirit
overtakes its innate ecstasis and becomes one
with it. But man can also dissemble his dependence on God, close in upon himself, "take

scandal" at his innate poverty. The temptation to do this is great. The radical indigence of our humanity has something repulsive about it. It devastates man, tears down self-created defenses and jars him out of the familiar, routine horizon of everyday life.

All too easily, man lives alienated from the truth of his Being. The threatening "nothingness" of his poor infinity and infinite poverty drives him hither and thither among the distractions of everyday cares. He runs away from the "night," with its fear and trembling before the truth of his Being, into the bright lights of easily understood platitudes. St. Paul termed this as seeking the security of the "Law," a security that distorts the elusive mystery and open authenticity of his Being. The Bible calls "Pharisees" those who try to evade the depth of their innate poverty through clinging to the "Law." They are "rich in spirit" and the most dangerous opponents of poverty, and hence of Jesus, because they vaunt their own brand of piety and seek to set up God as an opponent of poverty.

Left alone to himself, man still remains the prisoner of his own Being. He cannot successfully hide for long his mysterious Being. If he attempts this, the truth of his Being haunts him with its nameless emissary: anxiety. This becomes the prophet of the repressed mystery of his Being; with its alienation, anxiety takes the place of the scorned poverty. In the final analysis man has one of two choices: to obediently accept his innate poverty or to become the slave of anxiety.[1]

[1] On this theological interpretation of anxiety, see Johannes Metz, *Advent Gottes*, Sammlung Sigma.

The Poverty of Man Freely Accepted: Poverty of Spirit

We mentioned earlier that humble acceptance of our authentic Being is self-love in the Christian sense. In biblical terms it is "poverty of spirit". It is man bearing witness to himself, professing loyalty to his radical poverty, and shouldering the weight of self-emptying. It is man's consent to self-surrender.

In poverty of spirit man learns to accept himself as someone who does not belong to himself. It is not a virtue which man "acquires"; as such it could easily turn into a personal possession that would challenge our authentic poverty. Man truly "possesses" this radical poverty only when he forgets himself and looks the other way. As Jesus put it: "No one who puts his hand to the plow and looks back is fit for the kingdom of God" (Lk. 9, 62). To look back for reassurance is to try to acquire possession and full control over this virtue, which amounts to losing it.

Poverty can never be isolated from the roots of existence and laid hold of. It is thoroughgoing interiority. It is the concentrated commitment of all man's capabilities and powers. It cannot be viewed abstractly, it must involve total personal dedication. Like truth, it must be lived (cf. 1 Jn. 1, 16) from the depths of our heart, where our existence is unified and where our act of self-acceptance is unified and harmonized with our conscious presence to Being.

The fulfilled man is the one who dares to forget himself and to offer up his heart. "He who loves his life loses it, and he who hates his life in this world will keep it for eternal life" (Jn. 12, 25). To be able to surrender oneself and become "poor" is, in biblical theology, to be with God, to find one's hidden nature in God; in short, it is "heaven".

To stick to oneself and to serve one's own interests is to be damned; it is "hell". Here a man discovers, only too late, that the tabernacle of self is empty and barren. For man can only find himself and truly love himself through the poverty of an immolated heart.

This self-abandonment does not work itself out as some vague mysticism, in which the world and human beings are left behind. It constantly adverts to human beings and their world. God

himself drew near to us as our brother and our
neighbor, as "one of these" (cf. Mt. 25, 40.45).
Our relationship with God is decided in our
encounter with other men. One of the non-
canonical sayings of Jesus is: "A person who sees
his brother sees his God."

The only image of God is the face of our
brother, who is also the brother of God's Son, of
God's own likeness (2 Cor. 4, 4; Col. 1, 15). Our
human brother now becomes a "sacrament" of
God's hidden presence among us, a mediator between God and man. Every authentic religious
act is directed toward the concreteness of God in
our human brother and his world. There it
finds its living fulfillment and its transcendent
point of contact. Could man be taken more seri-
ously than that? Is anything more radically an-
thropocentric than God's creative love?

The nearness of God and the nearness of man
run closely parallel in the Christian outlook, for
which the humanity of Christ is the direct mani-
festation of the eternal Father himself (cf. Jn. 8,
19; 12, 45; 14, 5-11). Love of neighbor, then, is
not something different from love of God; it is
merely the earthly side of the same coin. At their
source, they are one (cf. Mt. 22, 37-40; 1 Jn. 4,
7-21) : that is the startling and distinctive note
in the Christian message.

Hence, it is in our relations with our fellow

men that our spirit of poverty is preserved, that our readiness for sacrifice enables us to become truly men. It is in these terms that Scripture describes salvation and damnation. It is as if God had forgotten about himself entirely. In the judgment scene he is visible only in the visage of our fellow men. Blessed is the man who has served his fellow man and cared for his needs; cursed is the man who has selfishly disregarded his brother and rejected the light of love and fellowship. The latter, in trying to enrich and bolster his own self, had turned his fellow man into his enemy and thus created his own hell.

Poverty in spirit does not bring man from men to God by isolating these components into separate little packages: God—Me—Fellow men. (God can never be just one more reality alongside others.) It operates through the radical depths of human encounter itself. In total self-abandonment and full commitment to another we become completely poor, and the depths of infinite mystery open up to us from within this other person. In this order, we come before God. If we commit ourselves to this person without reservations, if we accept him and do not try to use him as an instrument of self-assertion, our human encounter occurs within the horizon of unending mystery. This openness to others can be enjoyed only in the poverty of self-abandonment; egoism destroys it.

The Concrete Shapes
of Poverty

To become a man as Christ did is to practice poverty of spirit, to obediently accept our innate poverty as human beings. This acceptance can take place in many of life's circumstances where the very possibility of being human is challenged and open to question. The inevitable summons to surrender to the truth of our Being suggests itself in many ways. Here we want to highlight the most important forms that our poverty takes, to show how our daily experiences point us toward the desert wastes of poverty.

There is the poverty of the average man's life, who is unnoticed by the world. It is the *poverty of the commonplace*. There is nothing heroic about it; it is the poverty of the common lot, devoid of ecstasy.

Jesus was poor in this way. He was no model figure for humanists, no great artist or statesman, no diffident genius. He was a frighteningly simple man, whose only talent was to do good.

The one great passion in his life was "the Father". Yet it was precisely in this way that he demonstrated "the wonder of empty hands" (Bernanos), the great potential of the man on the street, whose radical dependence on God is no different from anyone else's. He has no talent but that of his own heart, no contribution to make except self-abandonment, no consolation save God alone.

Related to this poverty is the *poverty of misery and neediness*. Jesus was no stranger to this poverty either. He was a beggar, knocking on men's doors. He knew hunger, exile and the loneliness of the outcast (so much so that he will judge us on these things: cf. Mt. 25, 31-46). He had no place to lay his head (cf. Mt. 8, 20), not even in death—except a gibbet on which to stretch his body.

Christ did not "identify" with misery or "choose" it; it was his lot. That is the only way we really taste misery, for it has its own inscrutable laws. His life tells us that such neediness can become a blessed sacrament of "poverty of spirit". With nothing of his own to provide security, the wretched man has only hope—the virtue so quickly misunderstood by the secure and rich. They confuse it with shallow optimism and a childish trust in life, whereas hope emerges in the shattering experience of living "despite all hope" (Rom. 4, 18). Sinful man really hopes when he no longer has anything of his own. Any possession or personal strength tempts him to a vain self-reliance, just as material wealth easily becomes a temptation to "spiritual opulence."

In contrast to the above forms, there is the *poverty of uniqueness and superiority,* which is the honor and burden of the great men in history. Each carried a secret in his heart that made him great and lonely; each had his own exceptional mission, which, because it was without parallel, offered him neither protection nor guarantee among other men. No one enjoys such responsibility.

Satan attacks this poverty in Jesus, this call to stand alone, deprived of companionship and community. Every secret makes one poor, especially when its enigma scandalizes others and is misunderstood. "Be like the rest of men," whispers Satan; "feed on bread, wealth and worldly prestige—like the rest of us." It is a temptation put also to each of us: to renounce the poverty of our unique, mysterious personality, to do just what "everyone else" does. We are encouraged to repress the painful loneliness and individuality that foreshadow the terrible poverty and desolation of death, to betray our mission whatever it may be—unswerving loyalty to

another person, an undaunted love, the un-
yielding quest for justice or the lonely call to
duty. "Don't rock the boat. Why make a nuis-
ance of yourself? Why not live from the daily
bread of compromise? When in Rome do as the
Romans— *vox populi, vox Dei!* You'll only be
overruled and shouted down, without getting a
word of thanks."

So the argument runs, urging everyone to the
average, thoughtless mediocrity that is veiled
and protected by the legalities, conventions and
flattery of a society which craves endorsement
for every activity, yet retreats into public anonymity. Indeed, with such anonymity it will
risk everything—and nothing!—except a genuine, open, personal commitment. Yet without
paying the price of poverty implied in such
commitments, no one will fulfill his mission as
a human being. Only it enables us to find true
selfhood.

Closely related to the poverty of individual
uniqueness is the *poverty of our provisional
nature as human beings*. This trait is deeply imbedded in our existence. As creatures in history,
we cannot rest in the security of the present.
Our life today does not stand still; it stands on
the foundation of a long past, to which there is
also a long future ahead. A contemporary philosopher remarked how "our origin continues as
our future." What the past has made us is yet

to come. The mysterious, intangible beginnings of our life become visible only at its end. Only in the throes of death do our childhood dreams find realization. The future is the unfinished destiny of the past.

Thus, to take possession of our past and hold it securely, we must face the risks of a future that is yet to be. Only by taking this risk do we conquer the wellsprings of our life and follow the law of our Being. Our historical present suffers from the poverty of provisionality. This is exemplified in John the Baptist, an image of our provisional existence if ever there was one: "I am not the one. . . . After me comes he who was before me (Jn. 1, 20-21. 27). I do not belong to myself; I am a stranger to myself, a no-man's land between the past promise and the still to come fulfillment. I have nothing to make me strong or rich. Everything within me strains forward, is set on edge in prophetic anticipation—what poverty a prophet endures!—of an intangible future, and I am to find therein my true self, the promised land of my Father."

Man is only too ready to hide the poverty and neediness of his existence in history. He does not like the risks faced by the prophet, the dire poverty of hope, the life of a person who finds his support in the intangible promise of a provisional present.

Jesus described this mentality when he spoke

of the man whose time "is always here" (Jn. 7, 6). For this type of man the present is something he can lay his hands on, the past is the familiar strain of custom running through the present, and the future is something carefully plotted out *in the present*. "He is shocked by the inadequacy and uncertainty of historical existence with its unanswered questions and desires. So he excludes this open dimension of existence from the horizon of his understanding and performance. He accuses the forerunner and prophet of being "the enemy of tradition," of idolizing the passing moment and so disregarding the past, the custodian of which he prides himself on being. He has no sympathy for the poverty and martyrdom involved in human incompleteness and man's provisional nature.

The prophet of a future promise is spurned and misunderstood. "Serve the law that has been handed down to us," say the people around him. In fact, he does remain true to the law of our historical heritage. In him the continuity of history is maintained. In his poverty and effacement, the threads of history are woven together and the truth of history emerges. He sustains the priceless secret of humanity for us, rescuing it from the sterile routine and illusory self-evidence of the habitual. His powerful witness challenges us out of a hardened, unquestioning acceptance of the present into the poverty of the provisional future. As a pioneer and pacesetter, he comes to men under many different guises —teacher, philosopher, statesman, doctor, writer, priest, etc. He moves closer to the mystery of our heritage, plunges into it and lets it close over him.

What about the person who rejects man's provisionality? He will betray the wellsprings of his past heritage and sever himself from them. He will deafen himself to the call and challenge of the present. Moreover, because all historical understanding bears a prophetic character, understanding the present demands of a man that he be in advance of it, that the range of his vision reach out into that distance where the horizon and frontier-line of the present is drawn. To use the legacy of the past as a means of self-aggrandizement is to succumb to mythology. Man isolates himself from the power of his legacy and chooses to operate within the boundaries of a transparent and manageable present. When set before the rather gaunt visage of a life that thrives on the mystery and complexity of history, this form of existence seems, at first, so much richer and "come of age."

This was the spirit which the pharisees cultivated among the Israelites. They used the past to bolster and support their own righteousness; the

promise made to Abraham became a piece of
mythology. Only John the Baptist recalled them
to their original heritage (cf. Eph. 1, 4). To become a man in history, one must succumb to the
poverty of our provisional nature. This holds
for mankind in its entirety and for each and
every man as well.

Our existence in history is marked by another
form of poverty as well: the poverty of *finiteness*. Through the transcendental expanse of his
spirit man lives in the open air, in the future
of unlimited potentialities. His task is not to
lose himself there, but to make something of
himself through them. He makes them his potentialities by his historically unique and ir-
revocable personal decision, through which he
finds a foothold in the thrust of his existence.

This very decision, however, reveals the poverty of man's existence. For it involves the sacrifice and surrender of a thousand other possibilities. His decision is effective only when he
accepts this risk of human poverty; otherwise,
he must fall prey to ceaseless experimentation.

The poverty of finiteness is also experienced
in another way. The moment of decision is not
always open to us, nor always repeatable. There
is an element of finality about it. There is a
moment (cf. Col. 4, 5; Eph. 5, 16), an hour (Jn.
2, 4) when opportunity knocks, when man can
integrate the elements of his life and make them

whole. By the same token, man may miss his hour, for it is not an ever-present one (cf. Jn. 7, 6-8) which he can, consequently, manage as he will. Even our special moment reveals our impoverished finiteness.

Poverty has many other visages in our life. Every stirring of genuine *love* makes us poor. It dominates the whole human person, makes absolute claims upon him (cf. Mt. 22, 37), and thus subverts all extra-human assurances of security. The true lover must be unprotected and give of himself without reservation or question; and he must display life-long fidelity.

Every *genuine human encounter* must be inspired by poverty of spirit. We must forget ourselves in order to let the other person approach us. We must be able to open up to him, to let his distinctive personality unfold—even though it often frightens or repels us. We often keep the other person down, and only see what we want to see; thus we never really encounter the mysterious secret of his being, only ourselves. Failing to risk the poverty of encounter, we indulge in a new form of self-assertion and pay a price for it: loneliness. Because we did not risk the poverty of openness (cf. Mt. 10, 39), our lives are not graced with the warm fullness of human existence. We are left with only a shadow of our real self.

Finally, there is the inescapable *poverty of*

death. It is the lodestone for all the various forms of poverty of spirit: the cutting loneliness of our own Being, the lonely resolve of loyalty, the apparent futility of our love, along with the other manifestations of poverty. All these others are merely the prelude and the testing ground for the critical moment of death. It is here that the truth of our being is judged irrevocably. In death we experience the great poverty of our human nature; in death we carry out our obedience to our human destiny, with all its uncertainty and critical decisiveness.

Death reveals the self-annihilating quality of poverty in all its fullness. Man slips away from himself entirely. His freely fashioned destiny is concealed and taken out of his grasp. In the obedient and suffering acceptance of these depths of powerlessness, man is left with only the power of self-abandonment. At this point poverty comes to full achievement. Its meaning comes to full clarity in the cry of Jesus on the Cross: "Father, into your hands I commit my Spirit" (Lk. 23, 46). Submission to the forces of one's own death-bound nature becomes obedient self-abandonment to the Father, a total commitment to the full power of faith, hope and love. In abandoning himself to poverty, man abandons himself to God—whether he consciously realizes it or not. Poverty of spirit becomes the doorway to an encounter with God and to immersion in transcendence.

Thus poverty of spirit is not just one virtue among many. It is the hidden component of every transcending act, the ground of every "theological virtue." Our infinite poverty is the shadow-image of God's inner infinity; in it, thanks to God's grace and mercy, we are able to find our full existence. We discover in its unremitting demands upon us the unmistakable interpretation of God's will. His is no arbitrary will that sweeps across our being without appeal to our freedom. It is within our very being that the claims of this will find their lettering. That is why the individual guises of this poverty are the possibilities bestowed on us by God, the opportunities enabling us to become real human beings. They are the chalice that God holds out to us; if we drink it, we allow his holy will to work on us.

To be sure, none of us drinks the chalice of our existence to the last drop. None of us is fully obedient. Every man falls short of the human nature entrusted to him. We are all compromised in our acknowledgment of the truth of our being and in our work of becoming men (since that original fault at the dawn of mankind) . We never fully grasp the image of our impoverished being. There is a rift between ideal and actual life, between the real thrust of our life and our actual life from day to day. We always remain a promise never quite fulfilled, an image only dimly seen through a mirror (1 Cor. 13, 9. 12). We always stand at "a distance from our own selves, never fully sounding the depths of that being called 'I.'"

Our eyes and heart give way before we experience the full poverty of death. We are mercifully spared from the ultimate horror. Only dimly aware of it all, we stride across the range of our destiny. We never plumb the full depths of our poverty because, even in the attempt to accept it and take it upon ourselves, we encounter our powerlessness. We are, to use the relevant theological term, concupiscent. Concupiscence—this is what measures the meagerness of our poverty.

Because of concupiscence, we cannot experience our impotence to the fullest. In contrast to the Son of Man, we do not experience the full passion of our existence and the bitter truth of our poverty. It is our "happy fault".

This ancestral refusal to face our lot is a standing temptation for man. It leads him to give way to the same attitude in his *free* choices and to reject the humanity he has been endowed with. This freely chosen refusal is the root of all human guilt, the acute temptation faced by mankind.

The Dregs
of Poverty: Worship

All the great experiences of life—freedom, encounter, love, death—are worked out in the silent turbulence of an impoverished spirit. A gentleness comes over man when he confronts such decisive moments. He is quietly but deeply moved by a mature encounter; he becomes suddenly humble when he is overtaken by love. A certain luster plays over the visage of a dying man.

As a man draws near to his real wellsprings, his thoughts become devout, his understanding mellows, and his words slacken. His judgment becomes reserved and his objectivity becomes reverent. Philosophy then becomes open and receptive, readily accepting and shouldering the poverty and uncertainty of our spirit. How explain the rise within our hearts and spirits of this wordless, empty, but deeply stirring piety? Why this withdrawal from the teeming marketplace of facile thoughts and racy interests into

this recollecting poverty of a deep, chilling still-
ness that invades every recess of our Being?"

The reason is that in such experiences the
moment of truth arrives (Jn. 2, 4); our life and
our being are revealed to us. We then glimpse the
ground of our existence; we then gaze into the
precipitous depths opened up by such experiences. At such moments we are brought, not
only in "thought," but in the totality of our
Being, before the great mystery which touches
the roots of our existence and encircles our
spirit even before it is brought home to us with
full force.

At such moments we begin to realize that we
are accosted and laid hold of even before we lay
hold of ourselves. We dimly begin to realize that
we are poor, that our power and strength are de-
rived from the wellsprings of invisible mystery.

With faith our fear and trembling find their
voice once again. With faith we turn to worship.
But our speech is now composed of bold words,
"God" and "Father", and fed by the consoling
mystery uttered by Christ: "No one comes to the
Father, but by me" (Jn. 14, 6). Worshiping in
"spirit and truth" (Jn. 4, 23), man no longer
bears himself with the swagger of the executive
who knows what is up and has all under his
control. He realizes now that he is quite under
the hand of Another, claimed and summoned

to service. Man is mistaken, however, if he ex-
pects to find in prayer a shelter from the over-
whelming force of mystery. It is precisely in
prayer that he will cease to perceive this mystery
as the distant horizon of his acutely developed
human sensitivity and begin to hear about himself its encompassing challenge and summons.
Mystery acquires in prayer an identity, a name.
What manifested itself as an anonymous presence in the deep stirrings of human emotion
reveals itself in prayer as "Emmanuel," as the
presence of God with us. So identified, this mystery gains a total power over the full sweep of
our human existence. Over the hidden depths
and transcending breadth of our spirit? Yes.
But that is not the limit of God's power over us.
Under a variety of names he is familiar here
even to those who reject him outright. In the
man who prays, the range of God's power runs
from the depths to the surface, right into the
course of everyday thoughts and decisions,
words and actions.

Man no longer has anything that would stand
aloof from the imperious appeal of this mystery,
no credentials of independence. In worship man
hands over even his poverty and pledges it to
this mystery of God's all-encompassing presence.
Human language achieves its deepest meaning
when man, standing before this mystery, utters

not the call of retreat from it, but of advance into it; when his word expresses not alienation from this mystery, but an affirmation of it and a growing commitment of self to it.

Only prayer reveals the precipitous depths of our poverty. Submission to it involves an awareness of someone else. We are so poor that even our poverty is not our own; it belongs to the mystery of God. In prayer we drink the dregs of our poverty, professing the richness and grandeur of someone else: God. The ultimate word of impoverished man is: "Not I, but Thou".

Only when man commits himself without reserve to the recognition of this "Thou" does he hear himself endlessly called to the full taking possession of that priceless, irreplaceable "I" whom he is meant to be. In the great hours of a man's life this "I" announces itself, not as achieved reality, but as the possibility man is endlessly called to realize. It is when man, in the poverty of his worshiping spirit, treads before the face of God's freedom, into the mystery of that impenetrable "Thou"—it is then that he finds access to the depths of his own Being and worth. Then he really becomes a man. In worshiping God man is brought totally before himself and to himself. This is the case since man is, after all, given to himself, called and gathered into the depths of his personal Being, by the address and appeal of God.

Thus prayer is the ultimate realization of man. Surrendering everything, even his poverty, he becomes truly rich: "For when I am weak, then I am strong" (2 Cor. 12, 10).